HOW TO
SPEAK FLOWER

HOW to SPEAK FLOWER

A KID'S GUIDE TO BUDS, BLOOMS, AND BLOSSOMS

BY MOLLY WILLIAMS
ILLUSTRATED BY MIRIAM BOS

RP KIDS
PHILADELPHIA

**"For Piper and Mattie—
and the new generation of curious minds."**
—M.W.

Running Press Kids
Hachette Book Group
1290 Avenue of the Americas, New York, NY 10104
www.runningpress.com/rpkids
@RP_Kids

Printed in China

First Edition: May 2023

Published by Running Press Kids, an imprint of Perseus Books, LLC,
a subsidiary of Hachette Book Group, Inc. The Running Press Kids name
and logo are trademarks of the Hachette Book Group.

The Hachette Speakers Bureau provides a wide range of authors for speaking events.
To find out more, go to www.hachettespeakersbureau.com or
email HachetteSpeakers@hbgusa.com.

Running Press books may be purchased in bulk for business, educational, or
promotional use. For more information, please contact your local bookseller or the
Hachette Book Group Special Markets Department at Special.Markets@hbgusa.com.

The publisher is not responsible for websites (or their content)
that are not owned by the publisher.

Print book cover and interior design by Frances J. Soo Ping Chow.

Library of Congress Control Number: 2022937067

ISBNs: 978-0-7624-7917-7 (hardcover), 978-0-7624-7918-4 (ebook)

1010

10 9 8 7 6 5 4 3 2 1

CONTENTS

WELCOME!

······

BIRTHDAY FLOWERS. VALENTINE'S DAY FLOWERS. SYMPATHY flowers. Flowers just because you care. Flowers because you can't figure out exactly what you want to say.

No matter the reason, there's something very special about sending and receiving flowers. After all, it's been happening for thousands of years! There is a flower for every color of the rainbow—and every shade in between. We give and receive flowers for all kinds of events and reasons, but have you ever wondered what these forces of nature are really saying?

You're in luck! In the pages of this very book, you will learn how every detail—from the color to the species—of a flower can communicate the simplest (or, in some cases, the most complicated) message.

No, this is not a gardening book. You won't find how to prep soil or plant seeds, but you will learn the history behind the most popular flowers and learn the language of flowers!

From Ancient Greece to the Middle Ages, and from the Victorians to today, flowers are given to symbolize love, celebration, friendship, and healing. Some flowers can even signify dislike or serve as a warning, depending on the situation. Whatever you do, don't underestimate the power of the language of flowers.

Don't believe me? Try giving someone a bouquet and see what happens!

So, what do you think? Are you ready to learn how to speak flower? There will be fun quizzes that determine your own flower power and easy-to-read charts for when you need a quick reference in a pinch. Interested in creating a garden to grow flowers that match your own spirit? You'll learn about that, too!

It's going to be a fun, colorful ride!

A MINI-HISTORY
OF SPEAKING FLOWER

FLORIOGRAPHY: A WAY TO
COMMUNICATE BY USING FLOWERS

FLORIOGRAPHY HAS BEEN PRACTICED FOR THOUSANDS OF years. Literally! The practice has been crossing the world and cultures since ancient times. Across religions, cultures, and regions, flowers are one of the most common ways to express feelings and emotions.

We give flowers for all kinds of occasions and, whether you realized it or not, if you've given someone a bouquet, you've participated in the practice of floriography!

While we don't know for certain who was the very first, we can trace the practice around the globe to many ancient cultures.

Fun Fact

Flowers didn't always exist. They first appeared roughly 140 million years ago. Before that, ferns and cone-bearing trees dominated the plant world.

In Japan, Samurai warriors used flowers on images of their family crests in a practice known as *hanaktoba*. In fact, all over southeastern Asia, flowers were used as symbols of enlightenment and wisdom. Lotus flowers symbolized love and unity, while lilies and orchids symbolized good fortune and joy. The color of the blooms also expressed different meanings: pink for celebration, red for a long life, and yellow for wealth.

These same lotus blooms and lilies were also important in ancient Egypt, where they represented the geography of the region. The lotus flower became a symbol for upper Egypt—as a representation of the harmony between both upper and lower regions of the country. Lotus flowers and water lilies represented rebirth and continued life after death because of how they open and close during the day and night. The image of a papyrus plant represented lower Egypt and its agricultural power. The plant symbolized productivity, as well as growth and replenishment.

In South America, the native marigold was—and still is—an important symbol of life and celebration. The Aztec name for marigold is *campasúchil*, or "the flower of four hundred lives." For the Aztecs, the marigold was used not only for its healing properties but also as a symbol to honor the gods. The same was true for the Mayans, whose priests would drink a tea of marigold blossoms before calling on the spirits. These rituals were also the distant origins of what we now know as Los Dias de Los Muertos. The distinct smell of marigolds is said to guide spirits, which is why marigolds are often used to line paths from graves to houses so that deceased loved ones can find their way back home during the celebration.

Eventually, floriography made its way to Europe by way of Turkey. In the seventeenth century the lower classes who couldn't read or write used flowers to communicate with one another. In 1718, a British politician's wife, Lady Mary Wortley Montagu, who was living in Constantinople, wrote a letter home to her friends about the "secret language of flowers" that was being used there. It was enough to start an entire trend within the British aristocracy.

As the trend progressed, folks all over western Europe became obsessed with communicating with flowers. This was convenient because, by the eighteenth century, world trade and colonialism meant that new plants and flowers were constantly arriving at European international ports. The availability of new blooms expanded the floral vocabulary and meant that people could routinely send bouquets with hidden meanings to one another.

THE VICTORIANS

During the nineteenth century Victorian era, society really went all in for floriography. In 1819, a French woman named Louise Cortambert published the first floriography dictionary under the pen name Madame

4

Charlotte de La Tour. It was called *Le Langage des Fleurs*, "the language of flowers."

Dozens of flower language dictionaries and reference books were published soon after and most included gorgeous illustrations to go along with the descriptions. In 1884, the most popular floral dictionary—*The Language of Flowers* by Jean Marsh and illustrated by Kate Greenaway—was published in London.

The problem, however, was that as more people wrote books about the topic, different authors started assigning different meanings to flowers. Imagine the confusion if two people used different dictionaries and wound up saying the "wrong" thing based on what their book told them was the meaning of a certain flower!

MODERN DAY

Today, we have many wonderful flower-based resources at our fingertips—a quick Internet search or a trip to the library—giving us access to the incredible history of floriography! Even though we're living in the twenty-first century, the symbolic meaning behind different types and colors of flowers is still very important in our world. Yes, we have plenty of ways to speak our minds, but using the language of flowers is still a meaningful way to communicate with those around you.

Whether you want to let a friend know that you're there for them during a hard time or you want to convey your feelings to a crush, there's a way to do it with flowers! We can express complicated emotions and feelings—both positive and negative—without being face-to-face with the other person.

Speaking through flowers is possible with a single stem or a large arrangement—there's no right or wrong way!

SYMBOLISM IN FLORIOGRAPHY

LOVE

| Camellia | Carnation | Dahlia | Rose |

FRIENDSHIP

| Sunflower | Sweet Pea | Bellflower | Alstroemeria |

GRATITUDE / THANKS

| Lisianthus | Lily | Hydrangea | Tulip |

CELEBRATION

| Iris | Gladiolus | Heather | Baby's Breath |

HEALING

| Chamomile | Jasmine | Lavender | Marigold |

Color Meanings in Floriography

RED
love, respect, courage

LIGHT PINK
grace, admiration, elegance

DARK PINK
gratitude, appreciation

ORANGE
fascination, pride

CORAL
pride, desire

PEACH
"believe me," sweetness

YELLOW
true friendship, happiness, joy

WHITE
innocence, loyalty

BURGUNDY
undying love, beauty

LAVENDER
grace, spirituality, respect

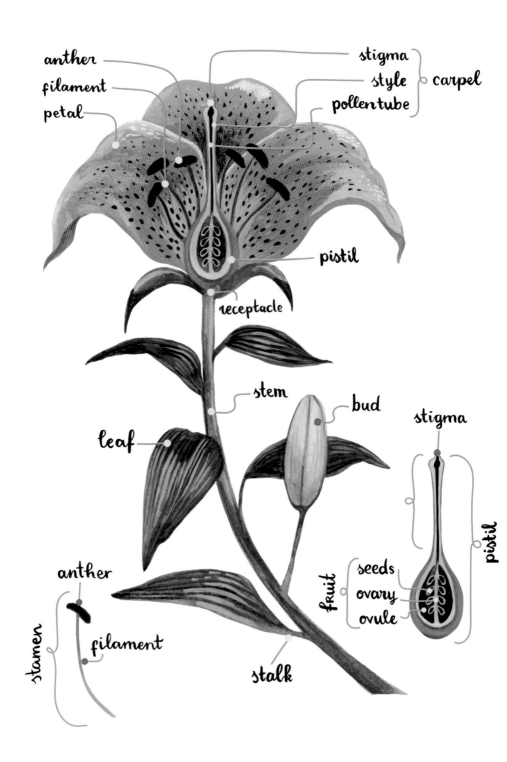

anther

filament

petal

stigma

style

pollen tube

carpel

pistil

receptacle

stem

leaf

bud

stigma

anther

filament

stamen

stalk

fruit

seeds

ovary

ovule

pistil

FLOWER PARTS:
Definitions

To understand all this business about flowers and their potential powers, you first need to know the different parts of the flower and how they all work together. Flowers can be found in a lot of different sizes, shapes, and colors, but almost all of them have the same basic structure.

Some parts of a flower help support the structure, while others give each bloom its distinct characteristics. Other parts of the flower perform specific functions for the plant to reproduce and survive another day.

Although flowers may seem small and simple, they're extremely complicated! Next time you get the chance, cut one down the middle and examine these individual parts. You'll be surprised by what you find inside!

ANTHER

The anther is the part of the stamen that produces the pollen. It is one of the most important parts for reproduction in flowering plants.

CARPEL

The carpel is another particularly important reproductive organ of a flower. Inside the carpel is the ovary, the stigma, and sometimes a style. There may be one carpel or a group of them.

FILAMENT

The filament supports the anther and helps it stay upright.

FRUIT

The fruit is part of the flowering plant that contains the seeds, which is key to the reproduction and life cycles. The fruit usually has a skin that is sometimes thin or hard. And sometimes fruits are mislabeled as veggies—like tomatoes, squash, and cucumbers. Those are all fruits!

LEAF

The leaf of a plant performs an important job. Its main purpose is to perform photosynthesis and gas exchange for the plant. Because of this, it is usually flat and thin so that it can absorb the greatest amount of light possible.

OVARY

This is the part of the plant that contains the ovules. Technically, it is the enlarged portion of the pistil. The style and the stigma sit right above it.

OVULE

The ovule is the structure that develops into a seed once it is fertilized.

PETAL

The petal is the colored part of the flower whose only job is to attract pollinators to the plant. Petals are modified leaves that surround the reproductive parts of the flower. All together they are called the *corolla*.

PISTIL

The pistil contains the stigma, the style, and the ovary of a flower.

RECEPTACLE

This is the part of the flower stem where all the parts of the flower are attached.

SEPAL

The sepals are modified leaves that are the first part of the flower to form. They protect the flower from drying out as it is forming. The sepal is also sometimes known as the bud.

STALK

The stalk is the load-bearing structure that supports the flower and is usually the entire body of the plant.

STAMEN

The stamen is made up of the filament and the anthers.

STEM

A stem is the structure that grows from the stalk to support the flower.

Fun Fact

The stem of a plant can greatly vary in size. Think of how different the stem of a flower is from the trunk of a tree!

STIGMA

The stigma is the head of the pistil. It is the sticky bulb that catches the pollen and starts the process of fertilization.

STYLE

The style is the long, thin structure that connects the stigma and the ovary.

PLANT BUZZWORDS

......

I F YOU WANT TO KNOW ABOUT PLANTS AND FLOWERS, YOU'LL have to know a few key words first. These buzzwords are all common lingo that will help you better understand the magical world of flowers and flower language.

ANNUAL

A plant that completes its life cycle, from germination to producing seeds, within one growing season. After producing seeds, it dies.

BEDDING PLANT

A decorative plant that is used in garden beds or containers when it is about to bloom. These are typically used only for a season and then thrown away.

Fun Fact
Flowering plants are complex, multicellular organisms with many distinct parts that have to work together to create a bloom.

BIENNIAL

A flowering plant that completes its life cycle in two growing seasons. Typically, the plant completes its growth in the first year and then produces flowers, fruits, and seeds in the second year.

CHLOROPHYLL

The green color that is found in chloroplasts. It absorbs energy from the sunlight and produces carbohydrates from carbon dioxide and water during photosynthesis.

CHLOROPLAST

The organelle in a plant cell where photosynthesis takes place. This is also the area that contains chlorophyll.

Fun Fact

The roots of a plant are used to absorb water and store nutrients, support the above-ground parts, and store leftover nutrients for times of drought or darkness.

CULTIVAR

A type of plant that botanists have bred for its desired traits, which are reproduced through controlled production. Most agricultural crops that are widely grown are cultivars, as are fruit trees, roses, and bedding plants.

CUT FLOWER

Flowers and other stems of foliage that have been cut from a plant for decorative use. To be used as a cut flower, the bloom must be able to have a decent vase-life.

GERMINATION

When a seed begins to grow. It also refers to the growth of a seed into a seedling.

LIFE CYCLE

Plants have a life cycle, just like humans and animals. The plant life cycle contains stages that the plant goes through from germination to the end, after it has produced seeds.

PERENNIAL

A plant that lives more than two years. This is a word that's used to tell the difference between plants that have a short, seasonal life and plants that can live much longer.

PHOTOSYNTHESIS

The method by which green plants (and, actually, some organisms) use sunlight to process nutrients from water and carbon dioxide.

ROOTS

The part of the plant that's buried in the soil. Roots hold the plant in the ground and help keep it upright.

Fun Fact

The leaves of a plant are used to capture sunlight to create energy for the plant through photosynthesis.

THE FLOWER LIFE CYCLE

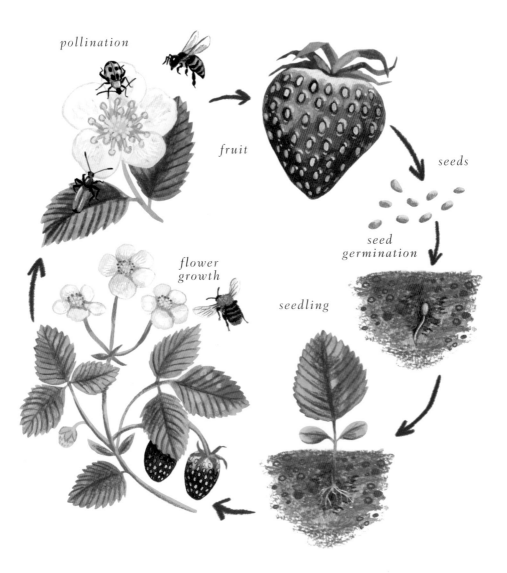

pollination

fruit

seeds

seed germination

flower growth

seedling

T HE FLOWER LIFE CYCLE BEGINS WITH THE LIFE CYCLE OF the plant—when a seed falls to the ground from its parent plant. There are all kinds of plant life out there, but flowering plants are the most common because of their ability to attract pollinators and spread their seeds all over the place. Flowers play a very important role in the reproduction of plants. Almost all the important stages of the life cycle happen because of the work the flower does.

There are six stages of the flower life cycle: seed, seed germination, seedling, flower growth, pollination, and the fruit.

SEED

All seeds hold a mini-plant called an embryo. There are two types of flowering plant seeds: dicots and monocots. The most common example of a dicot is a bean seed. It has two parts, called cotyledons, in addition to the embryo. The cotyledons store food for the plant.

Cotyledons are also the first leaves of the plant. They pop out of the ground after germination. Monocots, like corn seeds, have only one cotyledon. The hard outside of the seed is called the seed coat and it protects the embryo. Some seeds can grow after many years if they are kept cool and dry. Some seeds need to be wet to weaken the seed coat before germinating.

SEED GERMINATION

After a seed falls to the ground, it needs a few things to germinate. First, it needs warmth and water. Then, it needs light.

Dicots have seed coats that need to be wet to soften for germination. After the seed has been in the soil for a few days, it starts to absorb water, and then it swells up and the seed coat splits open. Monocots have a much harder seed coat that doesn't split as the seed germinates.

The stem that comes from the seed, called a *hypocotyl*, will push through the soil with the cotyledons (the first leaves, remember?) to complete the germination process. Some gardeners call it *sprouting*. The root system starts to develop, and the cotyledons fall off to make way for the true leaves of the plant.

Nature is truly mystifying. Some plants have adapted so that their seeds have to go through a specific environmental process before they can germinate. Some seeds, like prairie grass, need to be scorched or burned. Some seeds need to be scratched or scored. Some need to be eaten by an animal, digested, and pooed out before they'll germinate.

Every plant is different!

SEEDLING

Plants must produce their own food. It's a fact. For them to go through the complete life cycle, plants have to perform photosynthesis. As soon as green leaves pop from the stem, the process starts.

Plants contain chloroplasts in the leaves that convert energy from sunlight, carbon dioxide, and water into sugars, which they use as food. They store this food in the roots and in the stems and are eventually changed into energy used to make new plant growth.

Then, flower buds start to develop. Some plants flower within days of germination, while others take months or even years.

Fun Fact
Not all plants produce flowers. Plants like ferns use spores to reproduce.

FLOWER GROWTH

Inside the flower bud is a mini-flower form. The sepals protect the bud before it opens all the way. Over time the bud will open and the flower blossoms. After this happens, the sepals look like tiny green leaves at the bottom of the flower.

You already know that the flower is the reproductive part of the plant. The petals attract pollinators with their flashy colors and scent.

POLLINATION

After the pollen is caught, it travels down the style to the rounded part at the end, called the *ovary*, where eggs are waiting to be fertilized. The fertilized eggs become seeds. In fruit-producing plants, the ovary ripens and becomes fruit.

FRUIT

After the fruit is produced, the plant must disperse its seeds. After that step is complete, the entire cycle starts all over again!

POLLINATION 101

••●••

WHAT IS POLLINATION?

Technically, the act of pollination is the movement of pollen in a flower from the stamen to the stigma. Pollen is carried by insects, animals, wind, and sometimes even water. The smallest motion can trigger pollination. Some flowers even self-pollinate, which means that the pollen falls off the stamen and directly onto the stigma without help from any outside force.

There's also a process called *cross-pollination*, which is when pollen is transferred from the stamen of one plant to the stigma of a totally different plant. This means that the new offspring that is the product of pollination has two plant-parents instead of just one.

OKAY, THEN WHAT HAPPENS?

After the pollen has made its way to the stigma, the stigma starts firing off internal chemical signals to the rest of the plant. The pollen then produces a small tube that grows down through the style. This process allows the pollen cell to fuse with the cells inside the ovule, which successfully fertilizes the plant.

BUT WHERE DOES
THE FRUIT COME FROM?

After the plant has been fertilized, the fruit starts to develop. The ovule turns into a seed, which is surrounded by the ovary (this is where the fruit develops). Sometimes hundreds of seeds develop inside the fruit, but sometimes there are only a few. And—even more amazing—most of the seeds that are produced aren't viable to germinate and are useless.

Plants produce many seeds so that there's at least a small chance to produce a new plant.

HOW DO THE SEEDS
GET TO THE GROUND?

Seeds get to the ground through a process called *dispersal*. Naturally, the seeds need to germinate away from the parent plant (and each other!) because of the fierce competition for water and light. The seeds in fruits are dispersed in a few unusual ways—all of which are strikingly entertaining.

Water Travel

Most of the time, plants like purple loosestrife, mangrove, and plantain, which thrive near bodies of water, produce fruits that float once they drop from the parent plant. After they drop and take their maiden voyage, they eventually wash up somewhere and germinate.

Fun Fact
Most fruits have a sweet taste to help with the dispersal of seeds. If it tastes good to an animal, they're going to eat it and then eventually digest it.

Animal Poo

Animals eat fruit. That's just how the food chain works. Animals, like humans, have to relieve themselves at some point. The seeds bind with the animal's poo and are deposited wherever the animal feels the urge to relieve itself. Which, in nature, can be just about anywhere. Bonus fact: this is also how invasive species travel so quickly.

Wind

Some fruits are so small and light that they can eas-
ily get caught on a breeze. Some even have modified
structures that allow them to easily catch a ride on
the wind.

Solo Act

Many fruits split open as they dry, effectively launching the seeds into
the world.

Fun Fact

The scent, color, shape, and size of a flower is specifically created by the
plant to attract a certain pollinator.

Helping Hand

It's common that some fruits are covered in rough bristles
that stick to animal fur. Of course, the animal walks off and
takes the seeds with them. Eventually, the seeds fall off and
germinate elsewhere.

THE POLLINATOR CRISIS

It's no secret that the world is facing an extreme pollinator crisis. Entire populations of bees and other pollinators are seeing a drastic decline just about everywhere. There are reasons for this.

CLIMATE CHANGE

Many flowering plants are migrating to higher elevations to get away from warm temperatures. They're also slowly moving in a northward direction. Obviously, this is bad news. Not only does it impact existing ecosystems, but it also throws all these plants out of whack with their pollinators. Essentially, it becomes a big game of keep-away and the fight of the fittest plant. During this movement, many native plants and pollinators are displaced.

NON-NATIVE
AND INVASIVE SPECIES

Non-native species pose a big problem for native pollinators. Native pollinators need specific plants that provide very specific nutrition. Without it, these pollinators struggle to thrive and reproduce. Native plants and wildflowers are frequently pushed out by non-native and invasive species, which often do not provide pollinators with the quality of food they need. It's also possible for these non-native plants to attract non-native pollinators, which butt out those natives.

HABITAT LOSS

This might be the most obvious explanation for the pollinator crisis. Native pollinators need native plants and spaces. This is where they get their food in the form of pollen and nectar. These pollinators are genetically geared to thrive in native spaces, so when their habitats start changing or disappear, it's a big problem.

This problem is almost always caused by human development and alternate land usages. Not only does this take away a pollinator's food source, but it also takes away the space where they overwinter and nest.

AGRICULTURAL CHEMICALS
(PESTICIDES)

Chemicals have proven useful to the agricultural industry because they kill pest-insects, fungi, and weeds that destroy crops. However, they always affect pollinators in a negative way. Insecticides used on plants and plant seeds can hang around for a long time. It can affect the pollen grains that are a food source for pollinators by hurting or even killing them.

BOTANY VERSUS
HORTICULTURE

W E LIVE IN A WORLD OF PLANTS. THEY'RE EVERYWHERE
around us and provide us with many amazing things. From
food to fabric to building materials and medicines, we owe
plants so much!

You might know that a person who studies plants for a living is sometimes called a *botanist*. But what is botany? And how is that different
from horticulture? To really understand the difference between the two,
we must break each down into smaller pieces.

BOTANY: Botany is a broad class of science that deals with everything related to plants. It includes the study of plant physiology (how plants function), morphology (plant structure), ecology (how organisms relate to one another and the world around them), genetics (the variation in plant genes), and environment. Botanists handle the classification, distribution, and geographical importance of plants.

HORTICULTURE: Horticulture is a specific branch of plant science that deals with garden cultivation, plant production, cultivated ornamental plants, foods, and its management. Horticulturalists conserve the plants and related species and control the restoring process of a specific landscape. This all involves arboriculture, garden designing, and soil management.

Technically, botany is the scientific study of plants. Botany covers all the nitty-gritty details—structure to genetics to classifications. Botany is a science and botanists study plant life, from the smallest plant organisms to the largest, tallest trees in the world.

You'll find botanists working at arboretums, universities, pharmaceutical companies, and other biological companies. Usually, botanists specialize in one specific area of the science—and there are many areas! Some botanists have an ultra-specialization, where they study the plant life in a certain region of the world, like the Amazon rainforest or the jungles of Indonesia.

On the other hand, horticulture is more of an art form. By definition, it's the art and science of creating gardens and managing them. Horticulture is a branch off the botany tree and has to do with edible and ornamental plants. Where botany is a researched science, think of horticulture as an "applied" practice. You practice horticulture, often by using the research that has been done by botanists.

Quiz:
WHAT'S YOUR SOUL FLOWER?

1. The natural element you most identify with is:
   A. Air: I go with the flow, but don't mess with me or the people I care about.
   B. Fire: I am extremely passionate about life, but I also have a temper. Kind of.
   C. Water: I take care of the people I love, but I'm also pretty chill.
   D. Earth: I am one with nature and will stand up for what I believe in, no matter what.

2. What personality trait are you most interested in?
   A. Charisma: Good looks and a great sense of humor? Where do I sign up?
   B. Smarts: I'm all about identifying and solving the problem— every time.
   C. Emotions: There's nothing wrong with being in touch with my sensitive side.
   D. Determination: I work hard, no matter what, to get the job done.

3. Your best friends describe you as:
   A. Loyal: I'm the first one there after a bad day or to offer advice when someone comes to me with a problem.
   B. Ambitious: I'm always at the top of my class or the first to the finish line.
   C. Funny: I make everyone around me laugh, no matter what.
   D. Hard-working: I can do my homework and everyone else's chores before dinnertime.

4. When you're hanging out with a large group of people, you're typically:
   A. A wallflower: Wishing I could go hide in my room.
   B. Chilling: Two or three of my closest friends are all I need to chat with.
   C. Hosting: As in "the host with the most"—who needs more cookies?
   D. A social butterfly: I'm the life of the party, flitting from group to group and having a blast.

5. Your ideal day looks like:
   A. Reading: I'm finally starting that new book I've been saving for what seems like ages.
   B. Socializing: I'm hanging out with my best crew—whether it be walking around downtown or chilling at the local coffee shop.
   C. Hiking: I'm spending time outside. Maybe it's a long walk around the neighborhood or a short hike around the local lake—either way, I'm getting outside and I'm loving it.
   D. Entertainment: I'm either binging my favorite show(s) or waiting in line at the movie theater for the newest action film.

6. Your biggest strength is:
   A. Problem-solving: My friends come to me with their problems, and I can typically walk them through how to fix it.
   B. Inclusivity: I'm amazing at making others feel comfortable and included—no matter the situation.
   C. Planning: No matter what, I've got a plan. Whether it's for the upcoming week or the camps I want to go to during the summer, I've got it covered.
   D. Winning: I win, a lot. I win arguments and competitions and games. I'm a team player, but my drive is what helps me to the top.

7. Your favorite color is:
   A. Yellow
   B. Red
   C. Green
   D. Blue

IF YOU ARE:

Mostly A's: Sunflower

The sunflower is a hardy, reliable flower, just like you. You follow the light and enjoy weathering out the storm. When others give up, you'll still be standing.

Mostly B's: Lavender

You're a calming force to those around you. You're a loyal, steadfast friend and find joy in helping other people.

Mostly C's: Peony

You're emotional, and that's just fine! You like spending a lot of time outdoors, which can surprise some of the people around you. You also like to plan ahead.

Mostly D's: Rose

You're the life of the party, just like the rose. While you enjoy a good argument and winning the fight, you're devoted to those closest to you, and constantly remind them of what they mean to you.

FLOWER LANGUAGE: LOVE

INTRODUCTION

THE WORD "LOVE" DOESN'T HAVE TO MEAN ROMANTIC LOVE. There are all kinds of love! We can love our families, our friends, and people we look up to. The flowers and their meanings mentioned in this section represent the many varieties and shades of love—but of course this list isn't comprehensive. We have been giving all kinds of flowers as a symbol of love for hundreds of years—no matter what specific blooms are in the bouquets. Remember, it's all about the intention!

From true love to admiration and from a crush to showing your love for a family member, there's a flower for that! Let's see what they are.

CAMELLIA

The camellia is native to China, where it has a rich and diverse history. These flowers represent the union between two people who love each other eternally. A typical flower will lose its petals one by one as it dies, but a camellia's petals will stay connected to the calyx and will fall off together, all at once, representing long-lasting devotion and eternal love.

Camellias grow in the wild, and, depending on the variety, you can find camellias in shades of pink, red, and white. They grow on evergreen shrubs, and the gorgeous foliage is dark green with a waxy texture, which is a great complement to its massive, fragrant flowers. You'll find that some varieties will bloom during the winter months, while others bloom in the spring. But the most important thing to remember is that they bloom during cooler weather.

Symbolism

Camellias represent love, affection, and admiration. Each color has a different meaning!

Pink camellias represent a slow-burn type of love, or a love for someone who is missed. If you have a friend or family member who has moved away, sending them pink camellias would be a wonderful, heartfelt way of telling them that they are loved and that you are thinking of them even though they're no longer close by.

White camellias represent love between friends, or someone who is adored.

Red camellias represent true love.

Camellias can also symbolize deep understanding or patience during a difficult situation. If you have a friend who has recently lost a beloved pet and is having a hard time, sending camellias is a heartfelt gesture that will reassure them that you'll be there when they're ready to talk about it.

Camellia Fast Facts

- *Camellia sinensis* is used to make many green and black teas that are found in the average grocery store. Both the leaves and petals of this variety are extremely high in caffeine.
- There are only about three hundred different species of camellias, but more than forty thousand registered cultivars!
- The camellia is the state flower of Alabama.

CARNATION
Dianthus caryophyllus

Carnations are one of the oldest cultivated flowers in the world! Ancient Greeks and Romans were using them as decorations in their homes and temples way before they were given as Valentine's Day gifts. Carnations were used in Greece for ceremonial crowns and were known as the flower of the gods.

In paintings from the fifteenth and sixteenth centuries, you'll find carnations peeking out from bouquets in engagement portraits. These flowers are native to Mediterranean countries like Croatia, Greece, and Italy, but they can be grown in many different gardenscapes.

Symbolism

As floriography goes, different colors of carnations symbolize different things. Pink symbolizes gratitude while white carnations are a vote for good luck. Yellow can stand for rejection, but also friendship—so be confident in your intent. Purple can represent unpredictability.

Red carnations, of course, symbolize love and affection. This can be romantic love, but it can also mean love for anyone you are close to in your life.

Carnation Fast Facts

- Carnations are the most popular wedding flower in China.
- During the Victorian era in the late nineteenth century, carnations were used to send secret, coded messages to love interests. Sending any other color of carnation meant that the answer to a question was "yes," while sending a yellow carnation meant the answer was "no."
- Carnations are edible! They're not very tasty, but they do no harm! You can find carnations being used as garnish on wedding cakes, salads, and other dishes.

DAHLIA

Dahlias are an elusive beauty. They are native to Mexico, where they are the national flower. Hundreds of years before they were sought after for their beautiful bloom, dahlias were grown as food. The dahlia tuber (the part that grows under the ground, like enlarged roots) has a similar taste and texture to the sweet potato.

After corn and potatoes made their way across Central America, the dahlia became less important. That is, until Empress Josephine de Beauharnais of France started growing them in her garden in 1830. It was around that time that dahlias became known as a symbol for love and involvement.

The dahlia's versatile bloom doesn't travel well as part of the cut-flower industry, so if you want to give a bouquet of dahlias to the person you love, you'll have to find a local flower farm.

During the hot summer months, head down to a local farmers market and see if there are any flower farmers there selling their blooms. If you strike out there, a quick online search will put you in the direction of regional flower farmers who will be able to help you get your hands on some fresh-cut dahlias.

If you're handy in the garden and have the outdoor space, you can try to grow a few yourself! They're a great addition to the fall garden, which is their natural season for blooming.

Symbolism

Dahlias show love, involvement, devotion, and trust.

Dahlia Fast Facts

- There are more than forty-two official species of dahlias that vary in size and shape from pompons to dinner plates.
- Dahlias can be found in almost every color except blue.
- The dahlia is named after the Swedish botanist Anders Dahl, who researched the plant in the eighteenth century. Its original, Mexican name is *acocotli*.

ROSE

One of the most common symbols for love and romance, roses have been around since ancient times. They most likely originated in Central Asia, before spreading all over the northern hemisphere.

The rose is a type of flowering shrub that belongs to the family of plants called *Rosaceae*. Over thousands of years, it has been bred to produce dozens of different shades of blooms and to tolerate all kinds of growing conditions. Roses are a popular showcase plant in many gardens across the globe and are also prized as a cut flower.

Roses are one of the most common flowers to give if you're trying to convey love and affection. To create a bouquet with a little extra meaning, choose roses with specific color-coordinated meanings. And to top it off, add other flowers whose symbolism expands on your own feelings.

For example, if you want to send a loving bouquet to a grandparent, try a mix of red roses, sunflowers, chamomile, and irises to represent the love, friendship, and celebration that goes between a grandchild and grandparent.

Symbolism

Even though the rose has a universal meaning of love, different shades of different colors represent different kinds of love.

RICH RED: deep, bonded love and commitment

LIGHT RED: passion

PINK: admiration, young love, and the love of a friend

PURPLE: enchantment and love at first sight

Be wary of the intent behind yellow roses. Victorians used them as a symbol of jealousy, but these days yellow roses symbolize friendship.

Rose Fast Facts

- According to Greek mythology, Aphrodite, goddess of beauty, gave the rose its name in honor of her son, Eros, by rearranging the letters in his name. In time, Eros gave the rose to Harpocrates, god of silence, as a bribe to conceal the weakness of the gods. From there, the rose became symbolic of secrecy, silence, and love.
- The American Rose Society has more than forty different types of roses in its classification system—grouped into old world (before 1867) and modern (after 1867) roses.
- More than 250 million roses are harvested and sold worldwide each Valentine's Day!

FLOWER LANGUAGE: FRIENDSHIP

INTRODUCTION

NO MATTER WHAT KIND OF FRIEND PACK YOU RUN WITH—whether it's a crew of ten or just one or two close besties—friendship is important. These are the people who are here for you through thick and thin, no matter what. True friends stand with us through our toughest lows and our fantastic highs.

If you feel like celebrating your friends, try doing it with flowers! There are many flowers that represent the trials and tribulations of friendship, so the next time your BFF needs an extra hand, or you want to celebrate them "just because," try saying it with one of these flowers.

SUNFLOWER

Helianthus annuus

Sunflowers are known as one of the happiest flowers in existence. Who could get stuck in a bad mood when you have such a cheery face staring at you from your garden or favorite vase?

The sunflower is an annual flower, which means it needs to be replanted every year if you want these flowers continuously in your summer garden.

If you've grown sunflowers before, you might know that they always turn their heads to face the sun, no matter where it is in the sky. The sunflower is beautiful and iconic. It's a familiar face that also gives us so many by-products—like sunflower seeds and oil!

Symbolism

Many cultures and faiths have adopted the sunflower as a symbol. Over the years, it has represented faithfulness, harvest and bounty, and loyalty. Sunflowers also represent admiration and are frequently gifted as a good-luck gift among friends.

A handful of sunflowers given to your closest friend will brighten their day and relay how much they mean to you.

Sunflower Fast Facts

- The pattern of seeds within a sunflower follows the Fibonacci sequence, or 1, 2, 3, 5, 8, 13, 21, 34 . . . Each number in the sequence is the sum of the previous two numbers. In sunflowers, the spirals you see in the center are created from this natural sequence. There are two curves winding in opposite directions, starting at the center and stretching out to the petals, with each seed sitting at a certain angle from the neighboring seeds to create the perfect spiral. It's absolutely wild!

• Sunflowers are native to North America and have been traced back over five thousand years!

• Each sunflower has thousands of teeny flowers. The bloom of a sunflower is called a "head." The fuzzy brown center of the head is actually made up of individual flowers themselves. As many as two thousand can make up the sunflower bloom. The petals on the outside of the bloom are called "ray florets." The centers of the bloom are called "disc florets"—where the seeds grow!

SWEET PEA
Lathyrus odoratus

Sweet peas are a historical favorite in gardens and bouquets—and for good reason! They're known for their delicious smell and the way their petals grow, resembling butterflies.

Their scientific name means fragrant and attractive, which is very fitting for this flower! They are native to Sicily, southern Italy, and other Mediterranean countries, but they have been naturalized in many countries in the northern hemisphere.

These flowers are typically grown in gardens because of the sweet smells they give off. The distinct scent has been described as a combination of honey, jasmine, and citrus. It's a light, delicate smell that wafts on the breeze once the plant has fully bloomed in the weeks of late spring and early summer.

Sweet peas can be found in a variety of colors, from shades of red and pink to oranges and whites.

Symbolism

Historically, the blooms have been used for medicines and perfumes, but they became very popular during the 1800s as a decorative cut flower. During that time, the sweet pea became a symbol of new friendship and lasting loyalty—which translates all the way to the twenty-first century.

A bouquet of sweet peas is a great welcome gift to a new neighbor or a new student in your class who has just moved.

Sweet Pea Fast Facts

- During the Victorian era, the sweet pea was so popular that it popped up in all kinds of poetry and stories.
- In some cultures, the sweet pea is believed to have magical properties that will deepen one's wisdom and provide spiritual strength. It is often planted in yards in hopes of bringing joy, love, and peace.
- It is an annual climbing plant and can grow up to seven feet tall when supported.

BELLFLOWER
Campanula

The bellflower is native to Southern Europe and some regions of North America but can be found all over. Its common name comes from the flower's appearance, which looks like a bell once it's matured. Local folklore tells us that fairies planted bellflowers to trap children when they came across their path.

Now, bellflowers have become almost invasive in many places and are sometimes considered weeds. There are hundreds of different species that come in all different shades of blue and purple. Some varieties are tall and upright with large blooms, while others are smaller with tiny, dangling blooms. There is even a variety, *Campanula poscharskyana*, that has delicate star-shaped flowers. Depending on the species, bellflowers can bloom any time from early spring through late fall and are an important flower to pollinators like bees.

Symbolism

While the bellflower has symbolized many things over the years, from gratitude to love, friendship is one of its most popular meanings. The colors of the flower each represent something different.

CREAM: thoughtfulness, grace, and peace

BLUE: tranquility and friendship

PINK: joy, youthfulness, friendship, and happiness

Bellflower Fast Facts

- Greek legend states that Venus owned a magical mirror that reflected only beautiful images. When she lost this mirror, she sent Cupid to find it. Cupid dropped the looking glass and it shattered into a million pieces. True to its practice of making everything around it beautiful, the glass fell to the ground and sprouted stunning blue, bell-shaped flowers.
- Bellflowers can grow well in rock gardens, on a low wall, in a bed of perennials, in pots, or in planters.
- The bellflower is an easy plant to grow, which makes it perfect for a beginning gardener.

ALSTROEMERIA

Alstroemeria is one of the most common flowers found in bouquets, especially premade bouquets from your favorite grocery store or flower stand. They have a remarkably long vase-life and are inexpensive to grow, making them a favorite for florists everywhere.

Alstroemeria is also known as the Peruvian lily or the parrot lily. They are native to Peru, Chile, and Brazil and grow easiest in temperate climates. The stems are long, sometimes up to three feet in length, and the leaves grow upside down. Alstroemeria flowers have no fragrance, which makes them a perfect flower for those who have a sensitivity to certain smells or are allergic to pollen.

Symbolism

Over the years, alstroemeria has become a common symbol of friendship, particularly helping a friend through a difficult or trying time. The six petals of the bloom each have a meaning: understanding, humor, patience, empathy, commitment, and respect—all important elements of a true, lasting friendship.

Alstroemeria Fast Facts

- There are more than fifty species of alstroemeria and 190 cultivars that bloom in many shades of the rainbow.
- If alstroemerias get too hot, they will stop producing flowers.
- Alstroemerias bloom in the summer in Brazil and in the winter in Chile.

FLOWER LANGUAGE:
GRATITUDE

INTRODUCTION

THERE ARE SO MANY WAYS TO SAY "THANK YOU." GIVING thanks and showing gratitude not only helps us appreciate what we have been given, but it also helps us feel like we're giving back to those who have helped us in life.

Sometimes we need to go above and beyond simply saying "thank you" to someone. Sometimes we need to put a little more thought and care into the meaning behind the message. Picking flowers for a bouquet that have strong symbolism related to gratitude is a great way to show a little extra thanks to someone in your life who deserves it.

LISIANTHUS
Eustoma

Lisianthus flowers are well known for their long vase life, even though they look as delicate as crepe paper. Even though they're somewhat new to the flower circuit, these flowers have been around for hundreds of years. Lisianthuses are direct descendants from the North American wildflowers in the gentian family. In the wild, prairie gentian is known for growing in regions of Nebraska, Colorado, Nevada, and Texas. Also known as prairie gentian, lisianthuses have also naturalized in warmer climes like Mexico and the Caribbean.

Sometime in the 1930s, a Japanese botanist crossed a few flowers together to give us what we know as a lisianthus today.

A bouquet of lisianthuses can last for up to a month in a vase, which makes it the perfect gift to express your thanks for a teacher, mentor, or friend. Lisianthuses are also a great option for folks who like flowers on their desks or workspaces, so if you're looking for flowers to keep you company while you study, these might do the trick.

Symbolism

Lisianthuses generally symbolize gratitude and thankfulness—although the meaning can vary depending on the color of the bloom and the meaning you're trying to convey. Pastel pink represents grace and femininity. Yellow means happiness and joy. Green symbolizes a connection to the natural world. Deep purple conveys celebration and success.

Lisianthus Fast Facts

- Lisianthus flowers come in single and double forms, with double being the most popular.
- They're usually mistaken for spray roses.
- Because the name is a little tricky to pronounce, they're sometimes shortened to "lizzies."

LILY

Lilium

There are many, many flowers that take on the name "lily," but most of them are poseurs. To be a true lily, the plant must be a member of the genus *Lilium*. Yes, it's true—water lilies, daylilies, and arum lilies are all faux lilies!

There are somewhere between eighty and one hundred species of true lilies that grow all over the world, most commonly in Asia, Europe, and North America—places with warmer conditions. In their native environments, lilies grow in forests and grasslands as well as in the mountains. Thanks to botany and development, you can grow lilies just about anywhere now. Lily bulbs are extremely durable and can even be forced indoors in the cooler months.

As a cut flower they're long lasting and bring a pop of color or brightness to any bouquet. And, you know, this lily fad isn't a new thing. In fact, ancient civilizations *loved* lilies. The Romans used lilies to stuff their pillows (Ah! Very comfy!) and the Egyptians viewed lilies as sacred flowers that would connect them to the gods.

Symbolism

Lilies are great for all occasions and can represent many things, but if you want to show thanks, do it using yellow lilies. Yellow lilies symbolize joy and gratitude as well as friendship.

Lily Fast Facts

- Lilies are mildly toxic for dogs, but lethal to cats. A feline friend can die from ingesting any part of a true lily, including the pollen.
- Calla lilies aren't real lilies, either! They're part of the *Calla* genus.
- Throughout history, lily bulbs have been used, both fresh and dry, to treat inflammation.

HYDRANGEA

The hydrangea is part of the *Hydrangeaceae* family and a genus that has roughly seventy species of plants. There are hydrangeas that are as big as trees, hydrangeas that are perfect for a small pot, and everything in between. They're native to southern and eastern Asia and are famous for their vibrant colors.

The big blooms that these plants are known for are actually made of bracts, which is a modified leaf. The tiny little buds inside the bracts are technically the flower, not the entire thing on the end of the stem.

The name *hydrangea* comes from the Greek word *hydros,* which means "water," and *angus,* which means "jar." All of that makes sense because to successfully grow hydrangeas in your garden, you need to water them quite often!

Symbolism

Hydrangeas are fitting for any kind of heartfelt moment but especially when you're looking to show deep gratitude and thanks.

Hydrangea Fast Facts

- The color of hydrangea blooms is decided by the acidity of the soil.
  - Slightly acidic soil with a pH between 6.0 and 7.0 will create purple blooms. This pH also sometimes makes flowers appear as an ombre shade that slides between blue and pink.
  - Soil with a pH above 7.0 makes pink flowers. Sometimes this pH can even make red blooms!
  - If you have a hydrangea bush that has pink blooms, you can make them turn blue by adding aluminum to the soil. Add citrus peels, eggshells, and coffee grounds to the soil around the plant and the flowers will start to turn blue and purple.
  - If you want to change the flowers from blue to pink you have to decrease the acidity in the soil by removing the presence of

aluminum. The best way that you can do this is by sprinkling lime over the soil surrounding your plant.

- White hydrangeas are never affected by the pH level of the soil. They'll always be white!

TULIP
Tulipa

Did you know that tulips aren't native to the Netherlands? A lot of people think that they are because the country produces 4.3 billion tulip bulbs a year. However, tulips actually came from Central Asia! Explorers and botanists brought tulips to Turkey around AD 1000, where they got their common name, "tulip."

It wasn't until the sixteenth century that tulips were brought to western Europe—but no time was lost because, by the seventeenth century, tulips were so popular that they were being sold for five to six times their market value! At the time, tulip bulbs were more valuable than precious gemstones. They called it "tulipomania," and it's safe to say that the world never quite got over it, because tulips are still one of the most popular flowers in the world.

Symbolism

Tulips are a sign of spring! They're one of the first flowers to emerge after the winter and can bring smiles to everyone's faces—even after the longest cold months.

Tulips are also one of the most popular cut flowers and are some of the most affordable. Sending yellow tulips is a fantastic way to say thank you for a kind gesture!

Fun Fact
Several centuries ago in Holland, tulips were more valuable than gold.

Tulip Fast Facts

- Tulip buds are perfectly symmetrical.
- There are more than 150 species of tulips, and three thousand varieties.
- Tulip petals are edible! During World War II, tulip petals were used in all kinds of recipes, from wine to breads. The petals can even be used to replace onions!

FLOWER LANGUAGE: CELEBRATION

INTRODUCTION

O NE OF THE MOST EXCITING THINGS ABOUT LIFE IS THAT we get to celebrate the people we care about. And not just those big life-altering moments. Those small moments of joy and success deserve just as much recognition. What better way than to celebrate with flowers?

We celebrate things like getting over a sickness, having a new baby, or starting a new job. We can also celebrate moments like passing a big exam or finally dropping a bad habit. We celebrate life. These flowers represent celebration. Think about them as a symbolic "congratulations!"

IRIS

Iridaceae

The iris is a flowering perennial that is valued for its unique blooms and vibrant colors. The name "iris" refers to any of the three hundred species inside the genus that are all of varying sizes, shapes, and colors.

The iris first appeared in the gardens of ancient Egypt and were valued for their uses in perfumes and medicines. The flower eventually became a symbol of royalty in Europe—particularly in France. During the seventeenth century, King Clovis I added the iris to the royal banners as the fleur-de-lis, which went on to become a symbol for various royal houses all over the continent.

Symbolism

Because of the association with royalty, irises are frequently used as symbols of celebration. Purple irises, particularly, are used to celebrate almost any occasion, from birthdays to anniversaries to job promotions.

Iris Fast Facts

- The name "iris" comes from the Greek word for rainbow, which is also the same name for the Greek goddess Iris.
- The fragrance from the iris doesn't come from its bloom; it comes from its roots.
- The most common colors of irises are white, blue, purple, and yellow.

GLADIOLUS

The gladiolus is actually a relative of the iris and is in the same genus! It is also an example of a flower that is sometimes called a lily but is, in fact, a poseur. There are seven original species but more than ten thousand cultivars—which means there are plants out there of just about every size, color, and bloom shape that you can think of.

This flower is native to many places, including Asia, the Mediterranean, and South Africa. Its name comes from the Latin word *gladius,* which means "sword." Translated literally, the name means "little sword."

Gladioli (plural!) were often used for medicines. The plant's corms (the stem base that goes into the ground) were used to pull out splinters and thorns and also to treat colic in babies. However, many specific gladioli are poisonous if eaten—so never eat them!

Symbolism

These days, gladioli are used as bedding plants in gardens and as cut flowers in bouquets. These flowers are one of the best ways to celebrate an achievement. Their regal shape symbolizes honor and remembrance, making them a wonderful choice for the celebration of life for someone who has passed on.

Gladiolus Fast Facts

- An ancient name for the gladiolus was *xiphium,* which comes from the Greek word *siphons,* which also means "sword."
- Gladioli appear in many works by the great artists Claude Monet, Vincent van Gogh, and Georgia O'Keeffe.
- Gladioli are naturally resistant to parasites.

HEATHER
Calluna

Heather commonly grows in the northern and western parts of Europe, as well as in Turkey and Morocco. It's even been naturalized in some parts of North America. Its scientific name, *Calluna,* comes from the Greek word *kalluno,* which means to cleanse or adorn in celebration of good luck.

Heather is extremely popular in Scotland, where its common name comes from. It's widely believed that the word "heather" is derived from the Scottish word *haeddre,* which is often used to describe the shrubby habitat of the Scottish Highlands.

This plant is an evergreen shrub that does best in bright, hot sunlight. Depending on the region, it can bloom anytime from July to November and is frequently used in fall container gardening once the cooler temperatures set in.

Symbolism

Through the ages, heather has symbolized good luck, admiration, protection, and, most recently, celebration.

Heather Fast Facts

- Each heather flower can hold up to thirty seeds!
- In Scotland, during the celebration of a wedding, it's common for a bride to include heather in the bridal bouquet.
- Queen Victoria loved Scotland and, therefore, loved heather. She brought it into many royal celebrations and traditions.

BABY'S BREATH
Gypsophila

If you've ever seen a bouquet of flowers at a grocery store, you've definitely seen this flower. Baby's breath is one of the most popular flowers in the world for bouquets.

Baby's breath is native to areas of Asia, Africa, Australia, and Europe and is actually part of the same family as carnations. These little bitty flowers have five petals and can be found in white (the most common), pink, yellow, or light purple. They bloom in the summer months and provide a bounty of flowers, so much so that baby's breath is considered invasive in North America, where it is a big threat to native grasslands around the Great Lakes region.

Symbolism

Yes, baby's breath is common, but it's certainly not boring. In fact, the symbolism behind it is very emotional! The tiny blooms represent the delicate newness of a birth, which is why baby's breath is often given to new parents to celebrate the creation of new life!

Baby's Breath Fast Facts

- The *Gypsophila* genus is extremely diverse—there are more than 150 species of the plant, some of which are annuals and some that are perennials.
- The name *gypsophila* comes from the type of soil that the plant prefers. Baby's breath thrives in soil that is rich with the mineral gypsum.
- Because of the high saponin content in baby's breath, it is used in the production of photographic film!

FLOWER LANGUAGE: HEALING

INTRODUCTION

· · ● · ·

THE FLOWERS IN THIS SECTION DON'T SIMPLY SYMBOLIZE THE healing process—they also help it. These flowers have been celebrated for centuries for their health benefits. When used properly, they can impact your physical and emotional well-being and can be easy to incorporate into your life.

Remember, never, ever eat or ingest parts of a plant without talking to your adult and doctor first. Many flowers and plants look similar to extremely dangerous plants.

CHAMOMILE

This herb is native to Europe, Asia, and North America but has become naturalized all over the globe through trade. While there are many species of chamomile, we use only two of them. German and Roman chamomile are different in size and flower shape, which is how you can tell them apart.

Chamomile grows in a small, shrubby form, anywhere from a foot to three feet depending on whether you're growing the German or Roman species. Roman chamomile is an annual, but German chamomile is perennial.

Ancient civilizations like the Egyptians were the first to use chamomile in medicines. Chamomile is one of the most versatile herbs on the planet and is used in everything from perfume to medicines and teas. It has a delightful, warm smell that is often used for aromatherapy. Of course, not every beneficial effect of chamomile is scientifically proven, but it is used as treatment for many illnesses.

Symbolism and Usage

Chamomile is a natural anti-inflammatory, so it can be used to relieve pain and pressure from skin rashes, headaches, colds, anxiety, and other maladies!

It's also a great addition to any garden or cut-flower bouquet and can be a powerful symbol of health and healing. So if you have a friend who's sick or a teammate recovering from an injury, including some chamomile is a sweet way to say, "Get well soon!"

Chamomile Fast Facts

- The common fly is one of the main pollinators for chamomile flowers.
- Chamomile was one of the main herbs used during the mummification process in Ancient Egypt.
- Chamomile tea can be used to lighten your hair!

JASMINE
Jasminum

Jasmine is one of the most popular perennial flowers in the world! It belongs to a genus of vines and shrubs that contains more than two hundred species that are native to mostly temperate regions of Europe and Asia.

It's mainly grown for its flowers, which provide a powerful fragrance at night. Depending on the species, jasmine can be either evergreen or deciduous, losing its leaves when the weather cools in the fall.

The flowers are smallish and are often a shade of white. They grow in clusters, although some species develop flowers that grow alone. In nature, jasmine blooms during the spring and summer, but forcing jasmine to bloom in the winter has become a popular practice within the houseplant-loving community. Who wouldn't love a delicious-smelling plant in their home during the cold months?

Jasmine flowers release their signature smell at night, after the sun has gone down. It's also been said that the scent gets stronger as the moon begins to wax toward being full.

Symbolism and Usage

Tea made from jasmine flowers is said to have many health benefits. In ancient Chinese medicine, jasmine was used as an antibiotic and a fever reducer. It also has many calming properties, like chamomile. Jasmine tea is sweet and fragrant and one of the most famous teas in the world.

Gifting a jasmine plant to someone on the mend is a sure way to symbolize that they're on the path to full health.

Jasmine Fast Facts

- Jasmine flowers contain both stamens and pistils, so they can self-pollinate.
- Butterflies and bees are the main pollinators of jasmine flowers.
- Jasmine plants typically live fifteen to twenty years in their natural habitat.

LAVENDER

Lavandula

The scent of lavender is everywhere. There are candles, teas, perfumes, and potpourri. There's shower gel and essential oil and sachets full of dried lavender, too. It's even in desserts now!

Lavender is useful and versatile and has been linked to many health benefits for hundreds, if not thousands, of years. It's part of the *Lavandula* genus—a genus that includes about forty-seven plants. It can also be found all over the world.

It's been used as a tried-and-true remedy for many afflictions. The ancient Greeks used it to treat muscle pain and insomnia, and during the Dark Ages lavender was used to ward off the bubonic plague. Lavender farms in North America cropped up along with the Shakers, who sold it as an herbal medicine.

Symbolism and Usage

These days you can buy lavender dried, fresh, or as a potted plant. If you're looking for a plant to express a healing sentiment, lavender is the obvious choice!

These days, lavender is a common symbol of relaxation. If you have a friend who is stressed out about a test or upcoming theater production, giving them a dried sachet of lavender (or even an entire plant) is a wonderful way to help them de-stress for their big moment.

Lavender Fast Facts

- Lavender is one of the most effective natural bug repellents. It's naturally pest resistant and also protects the plants around it from infestations!
- Lavender is closely related to mint.
- Lavender-infused tea is frequently used to effectively treat upset stomachs.

MARIGOLD

Tagetes

Marigolds bring a bright pop of color to any garden or bouquet. They are part of the *Tagetes* genus and can be either annual or perennial depending on the species. Marigolds have dozens of layers of petals in each bloom, which makes them eye-catching!

Depending on the variety, marigolds can grow anywhere from a foot to three feet tall, with blooms spanning from a few centimeters to a foot wide. The varieties with longer stems are perfect additions to bouquets and arrangements. The flowers bloom in vibrant shades of orange, yellow, and red and bloom during the late spring through the first frost.

Many species are native to Central and South America, as well as Asia.

Symbolism and Usage

Like many other herbs, marigolds contain substances that have anti-bacterial, antiviral, and anti-inflammatory uses. Marigolds also contain lutein, one of the two major carotenoids found in the human eye.

Marigolds traditionally symbolize the strength of the sun and can represent the power and strength that we all carry inside of us. If you know someone who is feeling down or is facing an internal struggle, a bouquet of marigolds is sure to lift their spirits.

Marigold Fast Facts

- Marigolds can smell really bad. Depending on the species, they can have a musky, putrid smell. Don't worry, though; these days many varieties have been bred out of their stinky scent.
- The name *marigold* comes from the phrase "Mary's gold," the common name of the similar-looking flower *Calendula officinalis*.
- Marigolds are very important in Nepalese culture, and you'll be able to find them in almost every house.

FLOWERS WITH
NEGATIVE MEANINGS

We shouldn't bash a flower simply because it *might* have negative symbolism—mostly because the meaning behind flowers has so much to do with the intent of the sender—but there are a few blooms you should be aware of before giving them to someone you care about.

Here are some of the most well-known flowers that have some negative symbolism.

BEGONIA

"Bad luck"

Begonias are an extremely diverse group of plants with more than two thousand species and even more cultivars. They're beautiful, easy-to-grow plants. The flowers vary based on the variety.

However, if you give someone a begonia, you might be sending an ominous message. Begonias can be a way of wishing someone bad luck. They can also symbolize the desire to leave something behind. For example, if someone wanted to let go of a troublesome friendship, a begonia leaf or plant would be sent instead of having to tell the person to their face.

BUTTERFLY WEED

Asclepias tuberosa

"Leave me"

Butterfly weed is a species of milkweed native to eastern and southwestern North America. It is commonly known as butterfly weed because of the butterflies that are attracted to the plant by its color and scent! It's a species of milkweed that produces bright orange flowers.

The symbolism, however, isn't as cheerful as the flower looks. Butterfly weed symbolizes the desire to be left alone. Feeling salty? Send your siblings a bouquet of butterfly weeds to make sure they get the message.

YELLOW CARNATION
"Rejection"

We've covered that carnations can represent love and devotion, but it's important to understand the symbolism of the color. Yellow carnations famously symbolize rejection or a strong dislike for someone.

During the Victorian era, if a suitor was trying to win your affection, you could send them a yellow carnation to make it clear that you weren't interested.

CYCLAMEN
"Separation"

Cyclamen are popular plants that show up in garden centers around the holiday season. They have colorful flowers that brighten up any room during the darker winter months. It's possible for them to represent love and affection, but they can also represent the desire to be separated. Depending on the sender's intent, cyclamen can be a symbol for a breakup or the end of a friendship.

ORANGE LILY
"Humiliation"

Lilies can represent a lot of things. They're big, they're beautiful, and they're very popular. They also come in many different shades—from pink to white to maroon or orange. They're traditionally carried by brides and are a common staple in bouquets of all kinds. Orange lilies have become more and more popular over the years—and with that popularity, the negative symbolism has seemed to drop off.

However, for some, orange lilies can represent hatred, pride, and overall dislike—historically, sending them to someone was a way to let them know that you didn't like them or want their company.

PETUNIA
"Anger"

This ornamental bedding plant gives us blooms all summer long. It's one of the easiest annual plants to care for—all it needs is bright sun and regular water. It's a striking flower that makes a great addition to any hanging or window planter. But it's not very well known that petunias can symbolize anger and resentment. The flower became a passive-aggressive way for a person to tell the recipient they were mad at them.

DARK ROSE
"Tragedy or ill will"

As you know, roses can be found in all different colors, from the brightest of pinks to the deepest of maroons. There are some varieties of roses that are such an intense shade of deep maroon that they actually look black! These deep-colored roses are quite rare, and they can carry seriously negative meanings. Dark roses symbolize ill will or even tragedy—so be careful who you're handing them out to.

During the Victorian era, dark-colored roses became popular alongside the rise in popularity of Gothic literature. In those works, dark roses would often symbolize a doomed romance or foreshadow the death of a main character.

Fun Fact
Not all flowers smell good. One of the world's rarest, biggest, and smelliest flowers is the Titan arum, also known as the corpse flower.

DANGER:
FLOWERS THAT HARM

W E ARE NATURALLY DRAWN TO THE BEAUTY OF FLOW-
ers. At this point in our journey together, it's obvious! But
it's also important to remember that many flowers may look
harmless but can be poisonous.

In fact, there are plants that carry some of the deadliest poisons
known to mankind. There are thousands of toxic plants in our world, and
many of them are in our own gardens or backyards, and along roadsides.
One of the best ways to protect yourself is to know and understand some
of the most common poisonous flowers.

NOTICE:

IF POISONING OCCURS

The plants on this list are highly toxic, which means ingesting even a small amount of any part of the plant can result in symptoms of poisoning or even death. If you or someone in your home is experiencing poisoning symptoms, or if you suspect ingestion of poisonous plant parts, you *must* seek immediate medical attention by contacting your local emergency services or by calling the Poison Control Center at 1-800-222-1222. Do not try to treat poisoning symptoms at home, and never induce vomiting unless instructed to do so by a medical professional.

OLEANDER

Nerium oleander

Oleander is an evergreen shrub (sometimes it looks like a small tree) that has become a common ornamental plant in gardens. Gardeners love it for its unique funnel-shaped blooms (they smell delightful) and its ability to take a up a large amount of space in a small amount of time. It's fast growing and easy to care for, which just adds to its appeal as a landscape plant. Some oleander plants can grow up to twenty feet tall, and many have the capacity to grow just as wide.

What many people *don't* know is that all parts of the oleander plant are incredibly toxic and potentially deadly when ingested.

Oleander contains many chemical elements that can be toxic even when parts of the plant are dried. Ingestion of any part of an oleander plant can lead to a serious illness or even death.

ANGEL'S TRUMPET

Brugmansia

Angel's trumpet is part of the notorious nightshade family. You'll find it cultivated in frost-free regions and in many greenhouses across the world. These flowers are native to South America but are considered extinct in the natural world by the IUCN (International Union for Conservation of Nature) Red List of Threatened Species.

Angel's trumpet is an evergreen plant that branches out and can reach up to twenty-five feet high. The flowers are large and hang down toward the ground and can be white, cream, orange, pink, yellow, or red. Some species even have green flowers. These blooms have a very strong fragrance, particularly at night, and attract pollinators like moths and hummingbirds.

All parts of the plant are considered poisonous (even the pollen!) because they contain certain alkaloids like atropine. Any type of ingestion can cause disturbing hallucinations, memory loss, and paralysis, and can make the heart stop.

JIMSON WEED

Datura stramonium

Jimson weed can be found all over the world now, but it is native to Central America. It's also known as devil's snare, thorn apple, and devil's trumpet. It's a tall, herbaceous plant that contains chemicals like atropine that affect the brain and nervous functions on the body.

This plant blooms throughout the summer months and is frequently found in roadside ditches and fencerows. Jimson weed has thorny, egg-shaped pods that contain the plant's seeds.

All parts of the plant are poisonous, but the seeds contain the highest amount of dangerous atropine.

MONKSHOOD

Aconitum

Monkshood is a wildflower that has been naturalized all over the world. Also known as wolf's bane, the common name for the plant comes from its flower's resemblance to a hooded monk. It has a beautiful purple bloom that grows at the end of a tall stalk. It's also known as devil's helmet. Native to western and central Europe, it's commonly used in gardens as an ornamental plant and blooms in late fall.

Like others on this list, all parts of monkshood are poisonous, especially the roots and the seeds. The common name "wolf's bane" also comes from the historical act of poisoning wolves and criminals with the Europeans species of monkshood.

Monkshood has had its time in the spotlight over the years as a murder weapon. In 1881, George Henry Lamson was the first person to be convicted of using aconitine for the murder of his brother-in-law Percy John.

WATER HEMLOCK
Cicuta douglasii

Water hemlock is one of the most violent plants that grows all over North America. Only a small amount of the plant needs to be injected to induce fatal poisoning in the victim—including livestock and humans.

This plant has small, white flowers that grow in umbrella clusters. It's frequently confused with nontoxic wild carrots and parsnips. It's also confused with its relative poison hemlock, which can also be fatally toxic but has different toxins.

Water hemlock has pockets in its rootstocks that contain a severely poisonous brown sap. You'll find this plant growing in damp, wet areas of pastures, ditches, and streams.

CLEMATIS

The clematis is an extremely common flowering vine that's often found growing on a trellis in gardens all over the world. It's an easy, fast grower that blooms in many different shades of reds, whites, and blues depending on the species.

One of the most interesting things about this plant is that many people who have it in their garden have no idea how poisonous it is.

Clematis plants contain a chemical called *glycoside ranunculin* that causes severe pain in the gastrointestinal tract when ingested. If ingested in large amounts, clematis poisoning can be fatal. Most clematis poisonings are curious toddlers who are attracted by the pretty flowers and soft vines.

LILY OF THE VALLEY
Convallaria majalis

Lily of the valley is one of the most loved flowers of early spring. The blooms are delicate and fragrant and signal the end of a long winter. This flower is native to Europe and Asia but over the years has become one of the most popular bedding plants in North America.

All parts of this plant are toxic. In fact, it contains more than thirty cardiac glycosides, which affect the heart's ability to function. So, it's best to admire this delicate beauty from afar. If you do choose to add it to your seasonal cut-flower bouquets, use gloves!

FOXGLOVE
Digitalis purpurea

Foxglove is a plant familiar to those who love woodland and native plants. Originally native to Europe, it was brought to North America by cultivating enthusiasts. Once here, it escaped and is now considered invasive in some regions.

It grows wild along roadsides and fences where the soil is rich and fertile. It grows tall with spikes of pink, purple, blue, and white flowers. It has also become a common garden plant because of its eye-catching blooms.

Of course, it has earned its spot on this list because of its toxic cardiac glycosides. Eating any part of this plant will result in severe poisoning or even death.

Quiz:
WHAT'S YOUR FLOWER POWER?

1. It's the weekend. What are you up to?
   A. Enjoying my favorite book, again
   B. Hanging out with friends
   C. Going for a hike with the family
   D. Painting or writing

2. What do you worry about most?
   A. The people I love
   B. My future career
   C. My homework that I forgot to do yesterday
   D. I don't worry a lot, actually!

3. You're on a movie set! What's your role?
   A. The lead actor. Duh!
   B. The supporting role. Everyone needs support!
   C. The director. I'm always in charge.
   D. The costume designer. Someone has to make this all look good!

4. You're going on your dream vacation. Where is it?
   A. The ocean. Take me to the beach!
   B. The desert. Utah anyone?
   C. A staycation. Have you been to that museum yet?
   D. Abroad. I want to travel the world!

5. In a past life, you were probably:
   A. An explorer
   B. An artist
   C. Royalty
   D. A farmer

IF YOU ARE:

Mostly A's: Versatility

Flowers are versatile. They can be used as medicine, serve as homes or food sources for pollinators, and make beautiful decorations. Just as flowers can "do it all," so can you! You are multitalented, and your skills are useful in many, many ways.

Mostly B's: Strength

From the strength of roots to the hardiness of a seedpod, you have as much muscle as the strongest of plants—whether it be physical or mental. Don't let fear stop you from trying new things—you've got it!

Mostly C's: Resilience

Like flowers, you have the ability to weather anything life throws at you. Think of yourself as a plant that bends to the wind but pops back up stronger than ever. No matter what challenges come your way, you don't let them get you down. You always find a way to work through tough times and come out stronger and more confident than ever before.

Mostly D's: Disguise

Flowers like peonies and lisianthuses are deceptively hardy. Even though the blooms look delicate enough to crumble with the first movement, it's just a disguise. They really have a long bloom and vase-life. You're more capable than it appears on the surface. Whether you tend to be quiet or enjoy the spotlight, there's a lot that people don't know about you, and that's okay! We don't have to give all of ourselves to anyone.

DIY FLOWERS

NOW THAT YOU KNOW MORE ABOUT HOW TO COMMUNICATE with flowers, you can get creative with how you send your messages. Sending a single stem or traditional bouquet will always be a heartfelt gesture, but what if those flowers came from your own cutting garden? How much more would the act of giving flowers mean if you arranged the flowers yourself using your own bouquet recipe?

There are other ways to send messages with flowers, too! You can dry blooms and use the product to make bath bombs. You can even press flowers between the pages of a book to use in projects later. And of course, never underestimate the power of a flower crown.

HOW TO DRY FLOWERS AT HOME

● ● ◉ ● ● ●

When you dry flowers, you can save your favorite blooms for years. This is a great thing to do with flowers from a bouquet that are reaching their expiration point. Not only do dried flowers last decades longer than fresh bouquets, but you can use them in all kinds of crafts like homemade bath bombs and potpourri. You can also use them to make dried wreaths and bouquets to hang in your bedroom.

Drying flowers is really easy to do. All you need are a few supplies and your favorite flowers.

You'll need:

Rubber bands or string

Flowers

Scissors

Somewhere dry to hang flowers

STEP 1: Group your flower stems together and tie them with a rubber band or string. You can group as many together as you'd like, but they dry faster when bundled in smaller bunches.

STEP 2: Cut all the stems in the bunch to the same length. You can cut them as short as you'd like—this may depend on where you're going to hang them. You can always come back to this step and trim off a little more.

STEP 3: Hang your flowers to dry. Where you hang them is going to be based on what you have available that is out of the direct sunlight. Hanging flowers to dry in the direct sunlight will quickly fade the color out of the blooms and foliage.

YOU CAN hang them up on a hanger, a curtain rod, or even a nail on the wall. Wherever you choose to hang them, it needs to be sturdy enough to hold the bunch for a long time.

STEP 4: Wait for the flowers to dry. This step requires a lot of patience. You'll be waiting at least a month to see your flowers dry all the way through. Once they're dried, they'll be crispy and keep their shape when you hold them upright.

MAKING YOUR OWN
FLORAL BATH BOMBS

· · ● · · ·

*THIS CRAFT IS BEST DONE WITH AN ADULT.

Bath bombs are surprisingly simple to make at home, and they're a great way to use some of those dried flowers! These bath bombs are customizable, and you need only a few ingredients and supplies to make it happen. You don't even need a mold, because these can easily be shaped by hand.

You'll need:

Dried flowers

Citric acid

Baking soda

Water

Essential oil of your choice

BEFORE YOU GET STARTED MAKING YOUR BATH BOMBS, PREPARE THE FOLLOWING:

½ cup citric acid

1 cup baking soda

Water

Essential oil

Hand-crushed dried flowers

STEP 1: In a bowl, sift baking soda and citric acid together to make sure there are no lumps.

STEP 2: Add three to four drops of essential oil. Then, add the water a little bit at a time and stir until the mixture easily clumps together. Be careful not to make it too wet!

STEP 3: This is where you add your flowers! There are a few ways you can incorporate them into your bath bombs. You can add the flowers directly into the mixture and then form it with your hands into palm-sized balls. Another option is to form the balls immediately after adding the essential oil and water, and then roll them in the dried flowers. Either way works great!

STEP 4: After you've formed your bath bombs, let them sit out overnight to dry. In the morning, wrap them up for your friends or pack them up in an airtight container and store them somewhere cool and dry. When stored properly, bath bombs are good for up to six months!

FLOWER PRESSING 101

Pressing flowers is another easy way to preserve blooms and foliage for future craft projects. While hanging flowers to dry does a great job preserving, pressing them also flattens the bloom, which makes them perfect for scrapbooking or putting them into frames.

This craft is so easy that you don't even need an adult to help you. All you'll need are a few sheets of paper, a couple of heavy books or magazines, and the fresh flowers you want to press.

STEP 1: Before you get started, make sure your flowers are dry. Pressing wet or damp flowers doesn't work as well, and there's a chance they'll mold before they dry all the way.

STEP 2: Open your book or magazine toward the middle. To keep from damaging the pages of the book, put down a sheet of paper on each side.

STEP 3: Arrange your flowers on one of the sheets of paper. You can fit as many as you can, as long as there's a bit of space in between. Gently close the side of the book that the flowers aren't sitting on.

STEP 4: Figure out where you want your book to sit for the next month. Then, stack two heavy books or magazines on top of the book with the flowers in it. The added pressure makes sure that the flowers dry as flat as possible.

STEP 5: Wait! Pressing flowers typically takes thirty days or so. Try not to open the book to peek before thirty days are up—this could damage the flowers! Be patient. It's worth it.

HOW TO MAKE
HOMEMADE POTPOURRI

What exactly is potpourri? You might have heard an adult use that word at some point when talking about home decorations. The word *potpourri* comes from the French saying "pot pourri," which means putrid mud.

Kind of gross, right? But these days the phrase has made its way into the English language as "potpourri," and it refers to a mix of dried flowers, herbs, spices, and scented oils. Potpourri is usually displayed in a shallow dish and is used to make a room smell good. It also makes a great homemade gift and is easily customizable to the person you want to give it to.

Potpourri is simple to make at home with just a couple of supplies!

You'll need:

Large bowl
Mason jar (for packaging)
Orris root powder (to preserve the scent)
Essential oil of your choice
Dried flowers

STEP 1: Combine your dried flowers of choice in the bowl. Remember that potpourri is supposed to look as good as it smells, so it's important to think about the combination you're making. Think about color, size, and the intent behind each bloom. Do not crush the blooms; keep them whole and intact.

STEP 2: Add ten to twelve drops of essential oil around the flower mix. Don't just drip it into one spot. If you're making a larger batch of potpourri, you'll need to add more oil.

STEP 3: Gently toss the mixture in the bowl to spread the essential oil around.

STEP 4: Orris root powder is the official secret ingredient to know when you're making potpourri. The powder helps the scent from the oils bond with the dried petals. This is what makes potpourri smell good for such a long time. Add one to two tablespoons of orris root powder to your mix, and then gently toss it again.

STEP 5: Package your potpourri! Fill jars with the mixture and wrap them any way you'd like. Add a custom name tag along with the description of the potpourri to make it extra special.

CREATE A FLOWER CROWN

Fresh flower crowns are a fun and popular way to craft with blooms. They're great for any occasion, whether you're just hanging out, going to a concert, or attending a wedding. Flower crowns are simple to make (just four steps!) and even easier to wear.

Flowers That Work Great for DIY Crowns

LARGE: roses, zinnias, anemones, carnations, chrysanthemums

SMALL: statice, baby's breath, solidago, limonium, pom chrysanthemums

GREENERY: leather fern, ruscus, dusty miller, eucalyptus, cocculus

You'll need:

Fresh flowers:
Cut the stems of the flowers to about 3 inches to make it easy
to assemble. A mix of larger and smaller blooms along
with some greenery will make an awesome flower crown.
Remember that some flowers last longer than others when taken
out of their water source. See below for ideas!

Floral tape:
Used for wrapping fresh flowers together in little bundles
to attach to the crown. This tape is green and will easily blend in
with the blooms. It will also secure the flowers to the base.

Pipe cleaners:
This will be the base of the crown.

Scissors:
Use these to cut the flowers, tape, and pipe cleaners if needed.

STEP 1: Take the pipe cleaners and link them together until they fit around the crown of your head comfortably. Leave a little wiggle room and then cut off the excess pipe cleaner or wrap the ends around each other. Wrap the joint section with floral tape.

STEP 2: Wrap the greens around the base of the crown. Secure the greens to the pipe cleaners with floral tape. More greens equal a fuller flower crown.

STEP 3: Make mini-bunches of flowers to attach to the crown. Start by wrapping three stems together with floral tape. Make sure you wrap the tape from the end of the stem all the way to the base of the flower to make sure it's secure. After you've made a few bunches, start attaching them to the crown with floral tape. The key is to attach the flowers so that they're tight to the crown and don't flop around when you walk. This might take a few practice tries. Don't get discouraged.

STEP 4: Continue attaching flowers until you're happy with how the crown looks! Stop every once in a while, and try it on. There's no right or wrong look for flower crowns. They're all fabulous!

HOW DO YOUR
FLOWERS GROW?

YOU'VE LEARNED ABOUT THE HISTORY OF FLORIOGRAPHY and how to speak the language of flowers. You've also probably started to gravitate toward different types of flowers based on what you've read so far. Have you ever thought about growing your own flowers? Whether you have an entire garden outside or just a small windowsill space, you can grow your own blooms!

GROWING YOUR
OWN CUTTING GARDEN

One of the best things about having a garden is being able to grow varieties of flowers that can be used in flower arrangements. Whether you have an entire yard or just a few containers on your balcony, you can grow a variety of blooms for your own cutting garden.

The best part is that growing this type of garden is totally customizable. You can choose to direct-sow seeds and watch them grow or purchase mature plants from a nursery during the growing season. If you choose to sow your own seeds, remember to follow the directions on the back of the seed packet for the best results.

Any of the flowers mentioned in this book can be easily grown in containers or in your garden! The flowers below are just examples that work great for cut-flower bouquets—but can be interchanged with any favorites.

FULL SUN

Zinnia

These are an old-school favorite that are perfect for beginning gardeners. They bloom all summer long and love hot, full-sun conditions. Zinnias come in all different shades of the rainbow.

Interesting varieties: queen red lime, Oklahoma salmon, and zinderella lilac.

Cosmos

These unique blooms have really fun, long stems. They're hardy, continuous bloomers that are the perfect addition to any bouquet. There are many different varieties—some have larger, attention-grabbing blooms and some have small, delicate flowers. The stems can get lanky later in the summer, so if you see your cosmos flopping over, try supporting them with a stake-and-string system from behind. Another option is to search out varieties that stay on the shorter side.

Cool varieties: chocolate for a dark brown, unique color; double click for a frilly bloom; and sonata for classic petals.

Purple Basil

While purple basil isn't a traditional flower, it's a really fun change of pace for bouquets (and also in the kitchen)! Let your purple basil bloom and use it in arrangements. The long, purple flower spikes create a really cool visual in any bouquet, or simply in a vase by itself.

It has a long vase-life when cut at maturity once bloomed and brings a delightful scent to your bouquets and home!

Snapdragon

Snapdragons are an old-time favorite. They grow on a spike with blooms that look like their namesake: snapping dragons. Snapdragon varieties come in many different colors—from the purest white to almost black. They're an easy grow in full sun. Plant a mix for a variety of colors or try heirloom varieties for unique flair.

Interesting varieties: black prince, twin peach, and chantilly purple.

PART SUN

Hellebore

Hellebores are a well-known perennial and a bit of a unique cut flower. They have stunning blooms that are usually a shade of mauve. Be sure to cut only once the petals have a firmness to them. These plants are spring bloomers, but you can enjoy the beautiful foliage all season long.

Aquilegia

These plants are native to meadows and woodlands of North America. The blooms resemble tiny, delicate stars. Aquilegia plants thrive in part sun and can grow up to twenty inches tall. While there are many varieties to choose from, the dwarf variety blooms are especially adorable in flower arrangements.

Interesting varieties: little treasure dwarf spur, blue-white double winky, and black barlow.

Astilbe

Astilbe has bright, fluffy blooms that are perfect for part-sun gardens and containers. These blooms add bright, vibrant color to any bouquet. Varieties come in colors from white to dark red to lavender. It is also known as false goat's beard or false spirea.

Lamb's Ear

This soft leaf is frequently used in arrangements by floral designers because of its velvety texture. The leaves look and feel delicate, but lamb's ear is an easy grower in a container environment. This plant is a two-for-one. When it blooms, the plant presents a lavender or purple colored spike which can also be used as a cut flower. Doesn't get any better than that!

FULL SHADE

Hosta

There are many varieties of hosta out there. Some are very large while some stay tight and compact. Dwarf varieties are perfect for containers, while the larger varieties are great for bedding plants. You can use both their leaves and blooms for cut arrangements.

Interesting varieties: mini mouse, blue mouse ears, and filigree.

Bleeding Heart

Bleeding hearts are great additions to any cutting garden. Not only are they fabulous landscape plants, but their foliage and blooms have a great vase-life as cut flowers. You'll find different varieties that produce blooms of all different shades. These plants will keep coming back year after year if you decide to overwinter it.

Coleus

Of all shade plants, coleus might be the most popular because of its wide variety of leaf colors and patterns. All the different color options make this one of the most versatile flowers. Like hostas and lamb's ear, you can use the foliage and the bloom for a cut flower.

Interesting varieties: dark sun chocolate, wizard rose, and exhibition marble.

ARRANGING CUT FLOWERS

Not everyone has space to grow their own cutting garden. After all, so many of us live in cities and urban areas with no yard or outdoor space. There are still ways to bring flowers indoors so that you can enjoy and connect with them—from grocery store blooms to forcing bulbs to flowering houseplants.

Whether you harvested your flowers from your own garden or bought them at a farmers market or grocery store, you can create a gorgeous arrangement with nothing else but fresh water, a sharp pair of scissors, and a vase. Arranging cut flowers, also known as "floral design," is a great way to connect with the blooms. The practice is also a very meditative art form and gives you a quiet time to reflect on your life!

There are, of course, a few tips that will help you on your design journey!

1. Clean your vase before you use it.

It might seem basic, but cleaning out your vase or jar with hot, soapy water can make a huge difference in how long your cut flowers last. This practice helps keep your water clean longer, which makes your flowers last longer.

2. Strip the leaves off your stems.

Take the time to remove any leaves, stems, or flowers that will sit below the water line in your vase. Any plant part other than the main stem that touches the water will start to decay and dirty the water, which messes with your flowers' vase-life.

3. Trim flower stems at an angle.

This isn't 100 percent necessary, but it's good practice to prepare all of your stems by cutting them at the length you need, but at an angle. Cutting stems at an angle gives the stem the maximum chance to absorb water. Flat-cut stems that sit on the bottom of a vase won't absorb water.

4. Use tape to help keep flowers in place in the vase.

If you have a vase with a wide or awkward opening, use transparent household tape to make a grid. Then, place the flowers in the grid to keep them from falling or sliding around.

5. Make sure your stems are in the water.

It might seem obvious, but make sure all your stems are sitting deep in the water of your vase. It's easy when you're moving the vase around for flowers to get pushed out of the water. Before you walk away, make sure all those stems are submerged!

6. Refresh your vase water every day.

This extra step can be easy to forget, but it's one of the most important if you want to get as much time out of your cut flowers as possible! Change the water in the vase every day and give the stems a fresh cut every other day or so.

Additional Tips

If you can, use seasonal, local flowers!

Also, because there's no official "rule book" for floral design, try using unexpected things found in nature. Berry branches, veggies, and bark are all things you can use in floral design.

Your floral designs are an extension of your personality! There is no limit!

BOUQUET RECIPES

There are so many flower combinations you can use to create bouquets with meaning behind them—the possibilities are almost infinite! But, because of this, it can be really overwhelming to choose what flowers to put in a specific bouquet.

Use these "recipes" to get started! These are flowers that you can find at any florist, grocery store, or farmers market. They'll get the imagination going, and, before you know it, you'll be ready to create your own bouquet recipes!

Fun Fact
Snapdragon flowers look like little mouths. If you squeeze the sides of the flower, the mouth will open, and it can "eat" things. When you release the sides of the flower, it will close again.

Flowers for Your Best Friend
Light pink roses • Sunflowers • White hydrangeas • Mint

Flowers for Your Grown-Ups
Red roses • Chamomile • Sweet William • Mint • Hosta leaves

Flowers for Your Grandparents

Lilac • Blue hyacinth • Yellow lily • Basil

Flowers for Your Crush

Astilbe • White peonies • Blue salvia • Pink tulips

Flowers for Your Teacher

Sunflowers • Zinnias • Basil • Hydrangea

Flowers for Your Neighbor

Iris • Hosta leaf • Dahlia • Cosmos

Flowers for Someone Who Is Sick

Basil • Black-eyed Susans • Snapdragon • Chamomile

Flowers for Someone Who Has Lost a Loved One

Marigold • Sweet pea • Blue salvia • Red roses • Magnolia leaf

FLOWERING HOUSEPLANTS

• • ● • • •

Flowering houseplants are another great option to give to people in your life and offer a way to bring flowers into your home if you don't want to mess with cut flowers or don't have an outdoor space to garden.

Houseplants can be maintained year-round and many continue to bloom for months out of the year.

LIPSTICK PLANT

The lipstick plant symbolizes the unexpected beauty in the world around you. Because the blooms appear very quickly, it can seem like they've popped up, unexpectedly, out of thin air. A lipstick plant is a great reminder that beauty can show itself anywhere, at any time.

Lipstick plants are fairly simple to care for, with dynamite payoff. The lipstick plant cascades over the lip of its pot and can grow meters long in the right conditions. Give it bright, indirect light and weekly watering. These plants can handle underwatering but will quickly deteriorate if regularly overwatered. They also favor humidity, so mist regularly. If you want your plant to bloom more often, don't replant it until you absolutely need to. Lipstick plants thrive when root-bound.

There are also many varieties to choose from—from Thai pink to black pagoda. Lipstick plants generally bloom in the late summer and early fall.

GARDENIA

Gardenias represent gentleness and innocence. Keeping them around is a way to remember to be kind and gentle even in stressful situations. The blooms have a strong, spicy scent that can fill a space the moment a flower opens. If you keep a blooming gardenia plant in your house, you'll be reminded of its symbolism even if you're in a different room!

Even though gardenias have the reputation of being difficult to grow, as with most houseplants, follow a few rules and you should be just fine. Gardenias need at least four hours of bright sunlight a day to produce blooms. Keep the soil moist to the touch, but don't let the roots sit in water. If there's extra water in the catch tray, try emptying it with a baster from the kitchen. Mist daily. Leaves will turn yellow and the plant will drop its buds if it gets too cold at night.

OXALIS "PLUM CRAZY"

Oxalis are thought to bring about good luck and symbolize joy and positivity. Yes, these are the same plants that are referred to as shamrocks and clover. There are many different varieties, but all carry the same symbolism. Many believe that oxalis plants will ensure good health and happiness each day. Remember, it's all about the intent and what you want the flower and plant to bring to your life—but a positive outlook is a wonderful thing. These would make a great gift for a friend who is trying out for a team or a school play. Maybe you have an older sibling getting ready to go off to college—this plant is the perfect way to bring them luck in their dorm room.

While all oxalis varieties are interesting to look at, "plum crazy" is striking. The leaves are bright pink and purple and the plant easily produces dainty yellow flowers that rise above the foliage. The shape of the plant resembles a typical grass clover, but the color shows us that it's a truly spectacular specimen.

HOLIDAY CACTUS

Holiday cacti can live for decades, and even centuries if taken care of properly. Because of this, they're a constant symbol of longevity and loyalty. After all, who wouldn't want a blooming plant that has the potential to hang with you for your entire life? Giving this to your best friend is a great way to remind them that you're besties for life!

Their flowers come in an array of shades from white to corals, pinks to reds. Different species bloom at different times of the year, from Thanksgiving to Easter and beyond.

FLOWERS THAT MAKE THEIR MARK: USING FLOWERS TO DYE FABRIC

Did you know that until the middle of the 1800s, plants were the only source of dye for fabrics? It wasn't until it was discovered that one could manufacture dyes in a laboratory that bright, vibrant colors became commonplace in the clothing world.

After the discovery, using plants and flowers to dye fabric became a bit of a lost art form. Lucky for us, this way of coloring fabrics is making a comeback, and it's easy enough for you to do it in your own house!

WHERE DO PLANT DYES COME FROM?

Natural dyes come from all kinds of places in nature. Flowers, veggies, bark, mosses, and seeds are all great sources for pigment. It's important to understand the historical significance of each source and the influence they have on our culture today.

100

WHAT FLOWERS MAKE THE BEST DYE?

While many plants can be used to dye fabric, we're focusing on flowers here! Which is great because you can grow these flowers in your own garden.

Yarrow (Achillea millefolium)

This perennial is a member of the aster family and is native to the northern hemisphere.

It can grow almost anywhere and can reach from one to two feet tall. The leaves look kind of like chamomile and it produces flat heads of tiny flowers. Simmering the flower heads will give you a yellow dye, but the stems and leaves hold pigment as well.

Black-eyed Susan (Rudbeckia hirta)

Black-eyed Susans are popular perennials in the garden but are also a wildflower that is native to North America. If you use the leaves and the stems, you'll get a yellow dye. Simmering the flower heads will give you an olive-green pigment.

Hollyhock (Alcea rosea)

Hollyhocks are a long-time gardener's favorite. Though it was originally native to Europe and Asia, hollyhock has been naturalized all over the world. This perennial blooms during the hot summer months and can produce blooms in shades of maroon, red, pink, purple, yellow, and green, depending on the variety.

The lighter-colored flowers produce a yellow to brown shade of dye, while darker flowers can give you anywhere from a shade of lilac to deep purple to light red.

Indigo (Indigofera tinctoria)

Indigo is one of the oldest, most documented plants used for fabric dyeing. The plant gives a deep blue dye that has been used for thousands of years. While the plant produces a pretty flower, when making dye, it's the leaves you want.

Russian Sage (Perovskia atriplicifolia)

Russian sage is a hardy perennial that grows in a bush form. It produces spikes of lavender-colored flowers that are far more prominent than the leaves. These flowers make a lavender to a dark purple dye.

Hibiscus

Hibiscus is native to many tropical regions. In colder climates, it's a popular patio plant that's grown in containers. The plant produces big, delicate-looking flowers that are popular in tea mixes. While hibiscus tea is popular, you can also use the blooms to make dye. You can use dark red and purple blooms to make a rich red dye.

HOW CAN YOU GET STARTED USING NATURAL DYES?

*DYEING FABRIC OF ANY KIND SHOULD BE DONE WITH AN ADULT!

If you've never used fabric dyes before, one of the best ways to dip your toe in is to order a natural fabric-dyeing kit. These comprehensive kits tell you everything you need to know about fabric dyeing and come with all the necessary tools, too.

There are also quite a few resources out there to teach you about foraging, gardening, mordants, and other technical details about using natural dyes. A quick Internet search or trip to the library will get you started!

Plants/Flowers
and the Colors They Make

ORANGE
carrots, gold lichen, onion skins, yarrow

BROWN
dandelion roots, hollyhock oak bark, walnut hulls, tea, coffee, acorns

PINK
cherries, red and pink roses, avocado skins and seeds,
hollyhock, hibiscus

BLUE
indigo, Russian sage, red cabbage, elderberries, red mulberries,
blueberries, purple grapes, dogwood bark

RED-BROWN
pomegranates, beets, bamboo, hibiscus (reddish flowers)

GRAY-BLACK
blackberries, walnut hulls, iris root

RED-PURPLE
basil leaves, daylilies, pokeweed berries, huckleberries

GREEN
artichokes, sorrel roots, spinach, peppermint leaves,
snapdragons, lilacs, grass, nettles, plantain, peach leaves

YELLOW
bay leaves, marigolds, sunflower petals, yarrow, St. John's wort,
dandelion flowers, paprika, turmeric, celery leaves, lilac twigs

WHY CONNECT
WITH FLOWERS?

ℓℓℓℓℓℓℓℓ

ONESTLY, WHAT'S NOT TO LOVE ABOUT FLOWERS? THEY are so versatile! We use them to decorate our homes, show our wide expanse of emotions, and cultivate meaning in our gardens. These blooms help us form meaningful bonds with the world around us—from our relationship with ourselves to our relationships with others. The importance of connecting with flowers is completely intertwined with the importance of connecting with your emotions.

After all, we can enjoy almost every part of a flowering plant. From the unique color of the bloom to the delicate scent, flowers stimulate our senses on a basic level. And once we understand the life cycle and the meaning behind these blooms, we can connect more fully with that wild part of us that comes from Mother Nature.

GET IN TOUCH WITH
YOUR EMOTIONS

Flowers mean many different things to many people, but one constant is their ability to trigger happiness. Just having flowers around the house in a vase can bring a sense of happiness to our lives.

Flowers also appeal to our senses, which activates feel-good brain chemicals called endorphins. These chemicals not only make us happy, but they're natural healers of the mind and impact your mood in a positive way.

The effect of flowers can be immediate! That's why we give them as gifts for all occasions and why it's a good idea to buy yourself flowers when you're feeling down.

Keeping flowers—even if it's just a fresh stem or two—in your living space can help trip those happy emotions every day. All kinds of scientific studies tell us that just having plants and flowers around us can naturally reduce stress and anxiety levels. Flowers like peace lilies, gerbera daisies, and the flower of the bromeliad plant help remove toxins from the air.

CREATE MEANINGFUL
CONNECTIONS

We bring our own experiences to relationships. Sometimes flowers help us bridge the distance between ourselves and others—even if the distance is just a couple of blocks away. Sending or giving flowers helps make up physical distance when we can't be with each other.

Send a bouquet to your relatives in another state or to a friend who moved to a new town. Reestablish a lost connection or strengthen a bond!

Giving or receiving flowers helps develop all kinds of connections between people. As relationships strengthen, our brains release oxytocin, the "love" or "bonding" hormone. This helps us feel closer to each other, especially during difficult times.

LEARN ABOUT YOURSELF

Having flowers around, and working with them in the garden, can help us form deeper connections with ourselves. Self-care is so important, and flowers are a great way to treat yourself and gain self-awareness. Learning how to design a small bouquet, practicing pressing flowers, or literally stopping to smell the roses are all acts of self-care.

Historical Meanings of Flowers

Remember, the meaning behind each flower has to do with the intent or purpose when giving it to someone. Meanings change and evolve over time and based on a person's interpretation!

ACANTHUS: fine art, artfulness

AMARYLLIS: pride

ANEMONE: forsaken

ANGELICA: inspiration

APPLE BLOSSOM: preference

ASTER: love, daintiness

ASTILBE: patience and devotion

BACHELOR'S BUTTON: blessed

BASIL: good wishes

BEGONIA: beware

BELLADONNA: silence

BITTERSWEET: truth

BLACK-EYED SUSAN: justice

BLEEDING HEART: romance, broken heart

BLUEBELL: humility

BUTTERFLY BUSH: let me go

CALLA LILY: beauty

CAMELLIA, PINK: longing

CAMELLIA, RED: passionate love

CAMELLIA, WHITE: I adore you

CARNATION: love

CARNATION, PINK: I'll never forget our love

CARNATION, RED: heartache

CARNATION, STRIPED: refusal

CARNATION, WHITE: innocent love, pure love

CARNATION, YELLOW:	disdain, disappointment, rejection
CHAMOMILE:	patience, healing
CHRYSANTHEMUM, RED:	love
CHRYSANTHEMUM, WHITE:	truth
CHRYSANTHEMUM, YELLOW:	slighted love
CLEMATIS:	mental beauty, mental health
CLOVER:	think of me
COLEUS:	beauty and fertility
COLUMBINE:	foolishness, comedy
COLUMBINE, PURPLE:	resolution
COLUMBINE, RED:	anxiety
COREOPSIS:	cheer
CORIANDER:	hidden word or meaning
COSMOS:	order and harmony
CRAB APPLE BLOSSOM:	ill nature
CROCUS:	cheerfulness
CYCLAMEN:	resignation, goodbye, parting
DAFFODIL:	regard, unrequited love
DAHLIA:	love, good taste
DAISY:	innocent, loyal love, secret keeping
DAYLILY:	motherhood
FENNEL:	flattery
FORGET-ME-NOT:	true love, good memories, remember me
GARDENIA:	secret love
GERANIUM:	folly, jokes, stupidity
GLADIOLUS:	strength, victory
GOLDENROD:	encouragement, good luck
HELLEBORE:	serenity and peace
HIBISCUS:	delicate beauty
HOLLY:	defense, happy home
HOLLYHOCK:	ambition

HONEYSUCKLE:	bonded relationships
HOSTA:	friendship and devotion
HYACINTH:	sport, games, playfulness
HYACINTH, BLUE:	consistency
HYACINTH, PURPLE:	sorrow
HYACINTH, WHITE:	love, prayers, faith
HYACINTH, YELLOW:	jealousy
HYDRANGEA:	gratitude
HYSSOP:	sacrifice, cleanliness
IRIS:	faith, trust, wisdom, hope
JASMINE, WHITE:	sweet love, friendship
JASMINE, YELLOW:	elegance
LADY'S SLIPPER ORCHID:	beauty
LAMB'S EAR:	childhood, innocence, purity
LARKSPUR:	open heart, lightness, pickiness
LAVENDER:	distrust, healing
LILAC:	joyfulness, youth
LILY, ORANGE:	hatred
LILY, WHITE:	purity
LILY, YELLOW:	happiness
LILY OF THE VALLEY:	sweetness, innocence, end of winter
LOTUS:	purity, enlightenment, rebirth
MAGNOLIA:	royal, noble, connected with nature
MARIGOLD:	healing, celebration of life, honor
MARJORAM:	joy, happiness
MINT:	virtue
MORNING GLORY:	affection
NASTURTIUM:	conquest, victory, patriotism
PANSY:	thoughtfulness
PAPERWHITE:	rebirth, renewal, spring

PEONY:	bashfulness, happy life, shame or humility
POPPY:	consolation
RHODODENDRON:	beware, danger
ROSE, DARK RED:	mourning, deep love
ROSE, PINK:	happiness
ROSE, RED:	love
ROSE, WHITE:	innocent love, worthiness
ROSE, YELLOW:	jealously
SALVIA, BLUE:	thinking of you
SALVIA, RED:	forever mine
SNAPDRAGON:	deception, graciousness
SNOWDROP:	innocence and sympathy
SUNFLOWER:	friendship, adoration
SWEET PEA:	pleasure, goodbye, thank you, new friendship
SWEET WILLIAM:	pride
TANSY:	hostility, war
TULIP, RED:	passion, declaration of love
TULIP, YELLOW:	friendship, sunshine
VIOLET:	watchfulness, modesty, faith
YARROW:	eternal love
ZINNIA:	friendship, lasting love

Quiz:
TEST YOUR KNOWLEDGE

1. What is the process in which pollen is transferred by insects to other flowers?
   - **A.** Pollination
   - **B.** Reproduction
   - **C.** Cultivation
   - **D.** Digestion

2. What kind of flower is the fleur-de-lis?
   - **A.** Rose
   - **B.** Iris
   - **C.** Dahlia
   - **D.** Carnation

3. Which small, white flower is commonly used to make tea?
   - **A.** Pansy
   - **B.** Spray rose
   - **C.** Chamomile
   - **D.** Tulip

4. Which country did the Dutch first get tulips from?
   - **A.** Canada
   - **B.** Brazil
   - **C.** Turkey
   - **D.** Japan

5. What name is given to the smaller flowers you find in a dandelion's head?

A. Florets

B. Roots

C. Fibers

D. Stamens

6. Which color of rose, which now signifies friendship, signified jealousy in Victorian times?

A. White

B. Red

C. Pink

D. Yellow

7. What is the name of the sweet fluid that insects drink from flowers?

A. Nectar

B. Pollen

C. Water

D. Perfume

8. Which flower is associated with ancient Egyptians?

A. Marigolds

B. Roses

C. Lotus flowers

D. Fuchsia

9. In the United States and many other countries around the world, which flower is traditionally given on Valentine's Day?

A. Rose

B. Tulip

C. Hydrangea

D. Lilac

10. The anther is which part of a flower?
   A. Pistil
   B. Stamen
   C. Filament
   D. Receptacle

11. Which aromatic purple flower is often used as a fragrance for body products and as an herbal medicine for relieving and promoting good sleep?
   A. Lisianthus
   B. Petunia
   C. Dahlia
   D. Lavender

12. Which tiny white flowers represent the delicate newness of a birth?
   A. Chamomile
   B. Lavender
   C. Baby's breath
   D. Carnation

13. Which flower's scientific name means fragrant and attractive?
   A. Jasmine
   B. Sweet pea
   C. Rose
   D. Lily

14. What are the two main pollinators of jasmine flowers?
   A. Butterflies and bees
   B. Caterpillars and worms
   C. Wasps and hornets
   D. Birds and bats

15. What flower can mean ill will or even death?
   A. Dark roses
   B. Lilies
   C. Butterfly weed
   D. Lilacs

ANSWER KEY: 1. A, 2. B, 3. C, 4. C, 5. A, 6. D, 7. A, 8. C, 9. A, 10. B, 11. D, 12. C, 13. B, 14. A, 15. A

How many did you get correct? Check out the results below to see how you rank!

13-15 CORRECT—FLOWER EXPERT. Your skills at speaking flower can't be beat! We'll count on you to teach your friends all about the language of flowers.

10-12 CORRECT—FLOWER PRO. You know a lot about the language of flowers and can use it to your benefit!

7-9 CORRECT—FLOWER CHILD. You clearly enjoy learning about flowers and the messages they can convey. A little more studying and you'll be on your way to being a flower professional!

0-6 CORRECT—FLOWER NOVICE. You're still learning, and that's okay! Keep at it and you'll pick up what you need to know about communicating with flowers in no time.

MOLLY WILLIAMS is a born and raised Midwesterner living in New England. Most of the time you can find her with her nose in a book or getting her hands dirty in the garden. She is constantly trying to find ways to make her two passions, writing and floral design, intertwine.

Illustrator and pattern designer **MIRIAM BOS** comes from the Netherlands. (Interesting trivia: Her last name is Dutch for "forest.") She loves creating art that brings a smile to your face. A big lover of nature, Miriam lives in Apeldoorn, a city that is surrounded by forest ("bos") and heide ("heath").